Apple garland

Apples and apple blossom worked in cross stitch and outlined in straight Holbein stitch form a central garland on this tablecloth. A single rosy apple has been extracted from the design and worked on the corner of matching table napkins. If you are nervous about starting a big project such as the tablecloth, begin with the napkins and these may inspire you to complete the set. Or you can use parts of the cross stitch chart given on page 20 – a sprig of apple blossom or a cluster of apples – to decorate the edge of a tablemat, the corner of a small curtain or a dressing table runner in an evenweave fabric.

▼ **Table set for tea** A cherished heirloom, this tablecloth and napkins is worked in cross stitch with a delicate garland of apples and apple blossom.

KEY

	pale yellow 727		light rose 894
	light yellow 307		pale rose 776
	gold 725		white
	yellow ochre 783		light green 907
	orange 970		green 470
	red 349		dark green 987
	dark red 304		brown 434
	rose 893		dark brown 801

Materials
For tablecloth
DMC stranded cotton
2 strands each pale yellow 727, light yellow 307, gold 725, yellow ochre 783, orange 970, red 349, dark red 304, rose 893, light rose 894, pale rose 776, white, light green 907, green 470, dark green 987, brown 434, dark brown 801.
hardanger fabric gauge 22 to 2.5cm (1in) not less than 135cm (53in) square

For each napkin
DMC stranded cotton
1 strand each pale yellow 727, light yellow 307, gold 725, yellow ochre 783, orange 970, red 349, dark red 304, white, green 470, dark green 987, brown 434, dark brown 801.
hardanger fabric gauge 22 to 2.5cm (1in) no less than 36cm (14in) square *plus* **tapestry needle** No 24 and **embroidery hoop**

▲ *Tablecloth chart This quarter section is repeated to form the garland centrepiece. Use the dotted outlines at each end as a guide to place the repeat. Each square of the diagram equals one stitch workd over two threads.*

USING AN EMBROIDERY FRAME

A large project such as the tablecloth is best worked in an embroidery frame or hoop which will keep the fabric taut while you are stitching. Frames and hoops come in a variety of shapes and sizes from floor-standing frames to small, hand-held hoops. For thicker fabrics use a hoop with an adjustable screw on the larger ring.

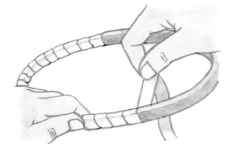

1 Preparing the hoop Bind the inner ring with tape to prevent it damaging the fabric.

2 Positioning the fabric Spread the fabric over the taped ring, then place the outer ring over the fabric, pressing down so that the fabric is taut, then tighten the screw.

3 Moving the fabric When moving the hoop, place a piece of tissue paper or muslin over stitches already worked to prevent damage. Tear or cut away the paper or muslin over the area to be worked.

HOLBEIN STITCH

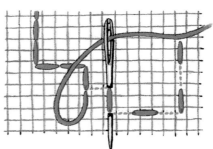

This is a simple running stitch used to outline areas of cross stitch and give it definition. Insert the needle from the back to the front of the fabric at start of the outline and work a running stitch around the motif. Return along the outline, filling in the missed stitches.

TO MAKE THE TABLECLOTH

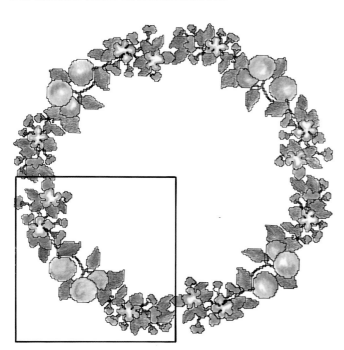

1 Mark the centre Fold the fabric in half and then into quarters to find the centre of the cloth. Use tacking stitches to mark the centre of the cloth along the folds.

2 Start to embroider Count the threads from the centre to the start of the design. Work in cross stitch (see instructions on page 10) using two strands of cotton. Each square on the chart represents one cross stitch worked over two double threads of fabric.

3 Repeat the section When you have finished the section shown in the chart, begin again, placing the first motif worked within the dark lines marked on the chart, until the garland is complete.

4 Outline the flowers Work Holbein stitch round the flowers as shown outlined on the chart using two strands of dark red 304.

5 Hem the edge Finish the cloth by stitching a double 2cm (³/₄in) hem with mitred corners.

TO MAKE THE NAPKIN

1 Hem the edge Turn a 1.5cm (⁵⁄₈in) double hem with mitred corners round the napkin. Tack and hem stitch.

2 Stitch the design Work a single apple motif in one corner of the napkin, positioning as shown on the chart.

3 Add a border Using two strands of dark green 987, work a line of cross stitch just above the hem through one thickness of fabric.

	727		304
	307		white
	725		470
	783		987
	970		434
	349		801

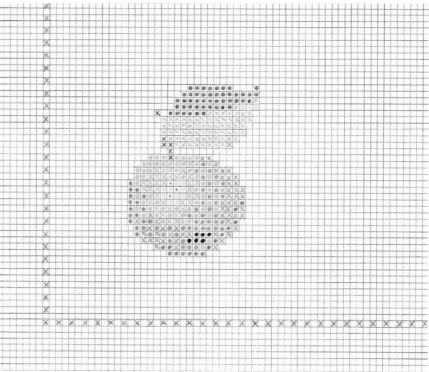

Rosehip table set

The embroidered jam pot cover and table napkin are cheerful accessories which will instantly brighten up your table. The set is made from fine aida fabric embroidered with a pretty rosehip motif in cross stitch. A simple border pattern completes the design.

▼ Red and white table set
Instead of aida you could work the motif on a purchased napkin.

Materials
For one jam pot cover
Anchor stranded cotton one skein each light green 239 and dark green 229
Anchor perle cotton No. 5 one skein each light red 46, red 13, dark red 47, brown 379, white 1
one tapestry needle size 24
fine aida 25cm (10in) square with 14 blocks to 2.5cm (1in)
narrow white lace 70cm (27¹/₂in) long

white cotton bias binding 80cm (31¹/₂in) long and 12mm (¹/₂in) wide
narrow satin ribbon in contrast colour 65cm (25¹/₂in) long to tie jam pot cover to jar

Additional materials for one napkin
Anchor stranded and perle cotton No 5 one skein of each of all the colours
fine aida 32cm (12¹/₂in) square with 14 blocks to 2.5cm (1in)

MAKING THE JAM POT COVER

The cross stitch embroidery is worked on a square of fabric which is then fashioned into an octagonal shape and the edges bound with bias binding and a purchased lace edging. A simple border pattern in cross stitch adds definition to the edge. Tie the cover on to the jam jar with a narrow satin ribbon.

1 **Find the centre point** Fold the fabric square in half and then half again. Press lightly and unfold. The folds can be clearly seen on aida; on a softer fabric, tack along the foldlines to mark the centre.

2 **Prepare the sewing threads** Split the stranded cotton in half and use three threads for the embroidery. Split the perle cotton in half and use one thread only.

3 **Stitch the motif** Work in cross stitch (see instructions on page 10) from the chart. Match the centre of the chart (marked with a black cross) with the intersection of the folded/tacked lines. Each stitch is taken over an intersection of single threads of fabric.

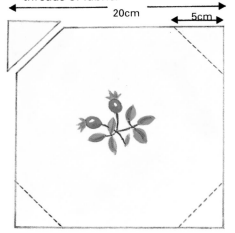

4 **Shaping the cover** Mark 5cm (2in) from each corner, along all sides of the square. Using the marks, draw a cutting line diagonally across each corner and trim off to make an octagonal shape.

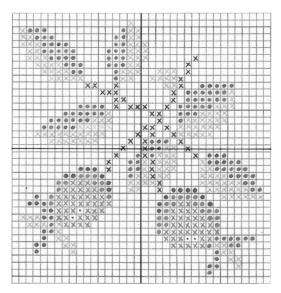

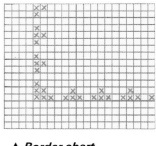

▲ **Border chart**
Each square of the diagram equals one stitch.

◄ **Motif chart**
Work in the centre of the jam pot cover or corner of a napkin.

KEY

⊠ light green 239	▦ red 13	⊠ light red 46
▦ green 229	⊡ white 1	▦ dark red 47	⊠ brown 374

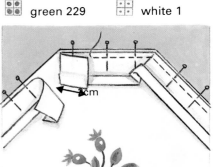

5 **Attach the binding** With raw edges level and right sides together, pin the bias binding to the edge of the fabric. Starting at one corner, fold back 2cm (³/₄in) binding and stitch along foldline to the corner, fold back at each corner to turn. At the end, overlap beginning of binding by 1cm (³/₈in) and trim off any excess binding.

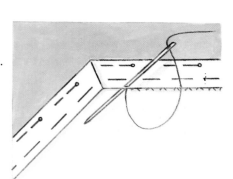

6 **Finishing the binding** Fold bias binding over to the wrong side, pin and tack, easing round corners. Slipstitch binding in place.

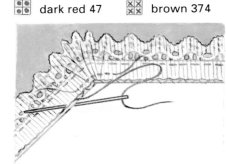

7 **Lace edging** Beginning and ending at a corner, pin right side of lace to wrong side of cover with the edge of lace along the hemmed edge of the bias binding. Gather lace slightly to ease round corners. Using a fine slipstitch, sew the edge of the lace to the edge of the binding.

8 **Border pattern** Work the triangular border pattern along the four longest edges of the cover, placing it 6mm (¹/₄in) from bias binding. Work a line of single cross stitches, placed one block apart, along the remaining short edges.

tip

Matching napkin
Work the motif in the corner of a purchased napkin or one made from aida. Work the border design along the hemmed edge, positioning the motif at least 14 blocks from the border.

Cosy chicks

Create a cheerful Easter breakfast with this colourful tea-cosy decorated with a hen and her chicks. Fluffy, yellow chicks are a traditional symbol of Easter and the ones depicted here are no exception – they are embroidered in yellow with bright orange feet, while the hen has brown feathers and a red comb.

The motifs are worked in cross stitch on an evenweave fabric and then the beak and wings are outlined in back stitch to give extra definition. Embroider the motif on the front of the cosy and either embroider the back or leave it plain. The matching egg-cosies have the same chick design, but these are designed as a smaller motif, which can be found on the left-hand of the chart.

To line the cosies we chose a smart brown gingham and picked a plain brown piping cord to outline the design.

Materials

White evenweave embroidery fabric with 22 threads to 2.5cm (1in), 80 x 50cm (31½ x 20in)

DMC embroidery cotton 1 skein each in the following colours: black 310, red 666, dark silver brown 840, chestnut brown 434, bright orange 741, light chestnut brown 436, silver brown 842, orange 742 and yellow 744

▲ Easter breakfast
Wake up to breakfast on Easter Day with these delightful hand-made cosies, which will keep everything piping hot.

Embroidery needle

Embroidery frame (optional)

Piping cord 90cm (1yd) of No 3

Bias binding in toning colour 90 x 1.3cm (1yd x ½in)

Gingham fabric for lining 70 x 40cm (27½ x 16in)

Mediumweight wadding 70 x 40cm (27½ x 16in)

Matching sewing thread

25

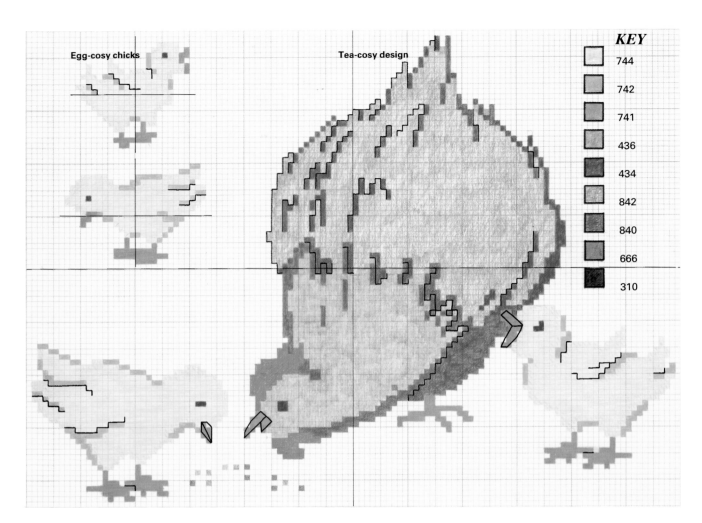

Egg-cosy chicks

Tea-cosy design

KEY

	744
	742
	741
	436
	434
	842
	840
	666
	310

MAKING THE COSY

1 Positioning the design
Cut two pieces of fabric 50 x 40cm (20 x 16in) for front and back. Oversew all round outer edges. Mark centre point along two adjacent sides of front. Tack straight lines from these points to form a cross that divides the fabric. The centre is where the tacking lines cross.

2 Working the pattern
Work the tea-cosy design in cross stitch, adding detail with back stitch. Match the bold black lines on chart with tacked lines, and begin working the embroidery in the centre, using two strands of cotton. One square on the chart equals one cross stitch worked over two threads of fabric. Work following chart and key.

3 Adding the details Then work the back stitch details, using one strand of embroidery cotton and following black lines on the design.

4 Cutting out Draw up the cosy pattern. Place centrally over the embroidered fabric and cut out, adding 1.5cm (⅝in) seam allowance all round. Repeat to cut one back, two linings, and two wadding pieces. Tack wadding to wrong side of main fabric.

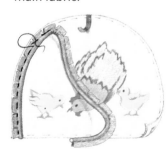

5 Making piping and tab
Make up covered piping to fit round curved edge. For tab cut a 7cm (2¾in) length of bias binding. Fold in half lengthways and topstitch. Place one raw end of tab to centre top edge of cosy piece. Tack piping round curved front edge, neatening raw ends level with base. Tack remaining end of tab over piping.

6 Stitching the lining Place white cover pieces with right sides together; pin and stitch curved edges catching in piping and tab. Pin and stitch curved edges of lining pieces together in the same way, leaving an opening in one side.

7 Finishing off Place lining over embroidered cosy with right sides together; pin and stitch all round base. Trim and turn cosy right side out through opening. Turn in opening edges and slipstitch together. Push lining up inside cosy.

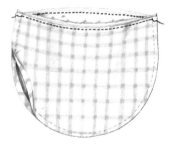

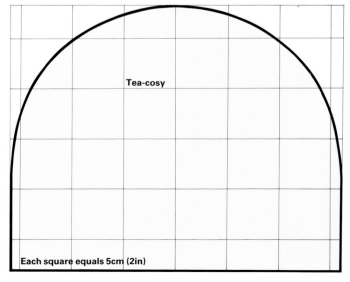

Tea-cosy

Each square equals 5cm (2in)

Pick of the bunch

This stylized floral picture would make a lovely starter project for someone who has never worked a piece of canvas before. The bunch of subtle raspberry pink and vibrant fuchsia flowers set against a punchy purple background gives the picture a contemporary feel.

The whole picture, which is only 17 x 13.5cm (6¾ x 5¼in) is worked in half cross stitch, with the main sections of the design outlined in back stitch to bring some form to the flowers. The flowers are framed inside a two-tone border of smoky grey and pink, highlighted with sharp muscat.

Should these colours not fit in with your decor, choose other colour tones. Even changing the background to a paler shade will make the picture look lighter.

If you have never stitched a piece of canvas before, it is an idea to practise a few half cross stitches on an off-cut of canvas to get the feel of the stitchery, so that your picture will look professional.

▼ Flower bouquet
Brighten up a dull corner with this vibrant embroidery. To complement the exciting colours, choose a simple toning mount and frame the picture with a bright red edging.

Materials
White single thread interlock tapestry canvas 35 x 30cm (14 x 12in) with 12 holes to 2.5cm (1in)
Masking tape
Anchor soft embroidery cotton two skeins of violet 112, one skein each of grey 235, raspberry 69, carnation 29, pale muscat green 278, muscat green 280
Anchor stranded embroidery cotton 1 skein of smoky grey 401
Tapestry frame
Milward International range tapestry needle size 18
Picture frame with backing board to fit

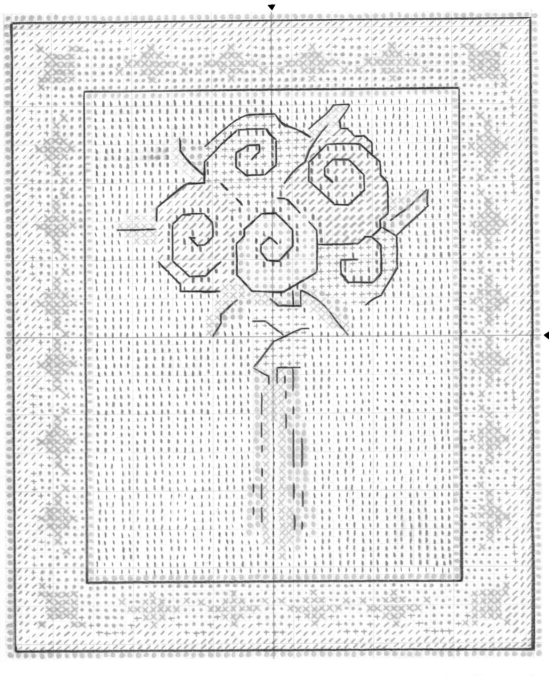

FLORAL PICTURE

1 Preparing canvas Fold masking tape evenly in half over the canvas edges to soften them. Tack across the centre of the canvas both ways to provide guidelines for the stitching. Set the canvas into the frame.

2 Following the chart The design is worked in half cross stitch using soft embroidery cotton and outlined with back stitch using three strands of smoky grey stranded cotton. The chart shows the design with the centre lines marked with arrows, which must match the tacked lines on the canvas. Each square represents one half cross stitch.

3 Working the canvas Begin the design centrally and work the picture following the chart and key for colours. When the half cross stitching is complete, outline the areas marked with a thick black line in back stitch. Remove from the frame. Steam press on wrong side, pulling canvas back into shape.

4 Mounting the picture Trim down the canvas to within 7cm (2¾in) of the worked picture. Mount the picture centrally over the backing board and frame as desired.

▲ *Each square equals one half cross stitch worked over one canvas thread intersection.*

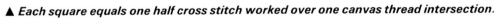

| ⊞ 29 | ⧄ 69 | ⊪ 112 | ⊡ 235 | ⊠ 278 | ⊡ 280 | ⊟ 401 |

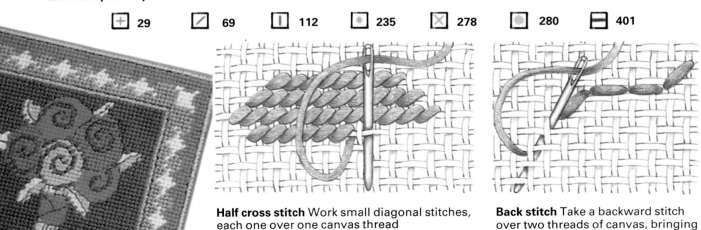

Half cross stitch Work small diagonal stitches, each one over one canvas thread intersection, as shown. If you are sewing correctly, the half cross stitches will be vertical on the wrong side of the canvas.

Back stitch Take a backward stitch over two threads of canvas, bringing the needle out of the canvas two threads in front of where the thread first emerged.

Summer cushion

This is the second of four cushion designs highlighting an individual season, and this is the pattern for summer.

The centre panel of this cushion features a bright orange and red poppy, which is surrounded by a border of blue flax flowers, and then a border of strawberry plants complete with fruit, flowers and leaves. Finally, there is a border of yellow wheat. The embroidery is mainly worked in cross stitch, and the finishing details are worked in French knots, with backstitch used to outline the flowers.

Each motif is embroidered in its true-to-life colours and all four cushions in the series have a plain white fabric background. Spring, Autumn and Winter cushions can be found on pages 15, 39 and 57.

▼ Lazy, hazy days
Make this season's delightful cushion and combine it with the winter and spring cushions for a perfect family. A brilliant red poppy is the central flower on this summer cushion. The bright blue flax, white strawberry flowers and red fruit in the surrounding borders give the cushion a truly summery feel, with a sunny yellow outer border.

MAKING THE CUSHION

Materials

Aida embroidery fabric 50cm (20in) square with 14 blocks to 2.5cm (1in)

Madeira embroidery cotton in the following colours and amounts: 2 skeins each of orange 0207, pale green 1310, yellow 0109; 1 skein each of emerald green 1307, grass green 1305, red 0210, dark blue 1008, medium blue 0911, medium green 1401, very pale yellow 0101, bright blue 1103, pale yellow 0112, bright yellow 0108 and dark tan 2009

Embroidery needle size 24

Embroidery frame (optional)

Backing fabric 43cm (17in) square

Decorative cord 1.80m (2yd) to match backing fabric or in one of the main colours in the embroidery

Sewing thread to match backing fabric

Cushion pad 40cm (16in) square

Note: Although it's usually effortless to work Aida embroidery fabric holding it in the hand, you will find it easier to work this design if the fabric is set into an embroidery frame. This has the advantage of leaving both hands free to work the stitches.

1 Marking the embroidery position Oversew all round the outer edges of the fabric to prevent fraying. Mark the centre point along two adjacent sides of the fabric. Tack straight lines from these points to form a cross that divides the fabric into quarters. The point where the tacking stitches cross is the centre stitch. The embroidery can be worked in the hand or set into an embroidery frame (see *Note* above).

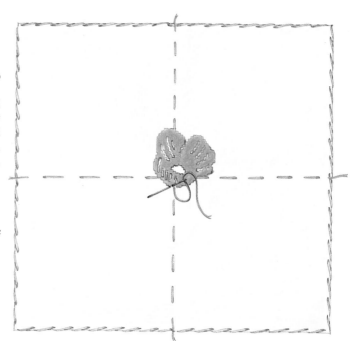

2 Beginning the embroidery Matching the bold black lines on Chart 1 on page 31 with the tacked lines, begin working the cross stitch embroidery in the centre of the fabric, using two strands of embroidery cotton. One square on Chart 1 equals one cross stitch worked over one block of fabric. Work the centre panel first, following Chart 1 for position of stitches and thread colours. Make sure the top half of the cross stitches face the same way. Work a border in medium blue 0911 all round the central motif. (For cross stitch see page 10.)

3 Working the borders Following the diagram left and Chart 2 on page 32, count the stitches and embroider the outlines of the three borders with one line of cross stitch, using yellow 0109 between the flax flowers and the strawberries, and medium green 1401 between the strawberries and the ears of wheat. Chart 2, on page 32, is turned 90° around the centre square to form the complete borders, as shown by the broken lines in the diagram left. Work the complete borders outwards from the central panel, following Chart 2 for the thread colours and placement of the stitches for flax flowers, strawberries and ears of wheat. One square on Chart 2 on page 32 equals one cross stitch worked over one block of fabric. Work the complete flax flower border first, then the strawberry border and finally, to complete the cushion cover design, work the border of wheat ears all round the outer edge of the cover.

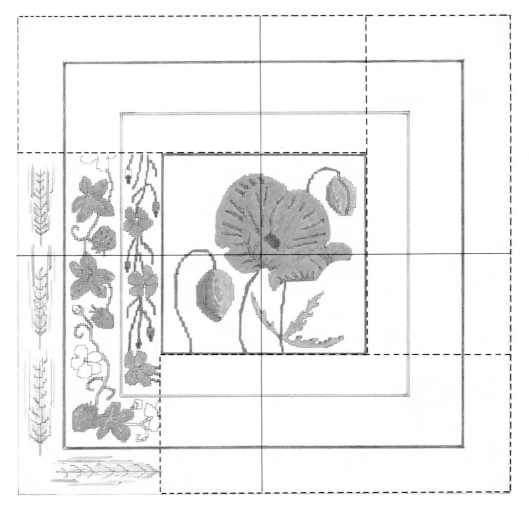

Chart 1

4 Adding details to the poppies
Work outline and details following marked lines on Chart 1. Use a single strand of dark blue 1008 to backstitch round the petals, following the dotted line on Chart 1. Use two strands of dark blue 1008 to backstitch the internal lines on the poppy, following black line on Chart 1. Work French knots in the centre of the main poppy flower head, using three strands of pale green 1310. (For details on working French knots see page 13.)

5 Outlining the borders Following the black lines on Chart 2, shown on page 32, use 1 strand of dark blue 1008 to backstitch the details around the flax flowers. Use two strands of grass green 1305 to backstitch the details on the strawberry flowers. Use a single strand of dark tan 2009 to backstitch the details on the ears of wheat.

6 Pressing the embroidery When the embroidery is complete, remove from the frame. Steam press on the wrong side, being careful not to flatten the stitches. Tack all round the outside to mark the outline.

7 Making up the cushion Trim down the fabric on all sides to within 2.5cm (1in) of the marked outline. Place to the backing fabric with right sides together. Pin, tack and stitch all round the cushion cover, leaving an opening centrally in base edge, for turning and filling. Trim sides and corners and turn cover right side out. Insert cushion pad. Turn in opening edges; pin and tack together.

8 Adding the cord Hand sew cord all round the seamline of the cushion. Tuck the raw ends of the cord into the centre of the tacked opening and pin together.

9 Finishing off Slipstitch opening edges together to close, catching in cord. Catch cord invisibly together at the opening.

KEY

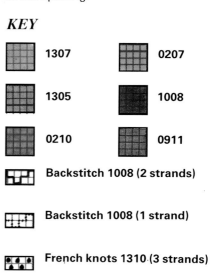

▨	1307	▨	0207
▨	1305	■	1008
▨	0210	▨	0911

Backstitch 1008 (2 strands)

Backstitch 1008 (1 strand)

French knots 1310 (3 strands)

31

CROSS STITCH EMBROIDERY

KEY

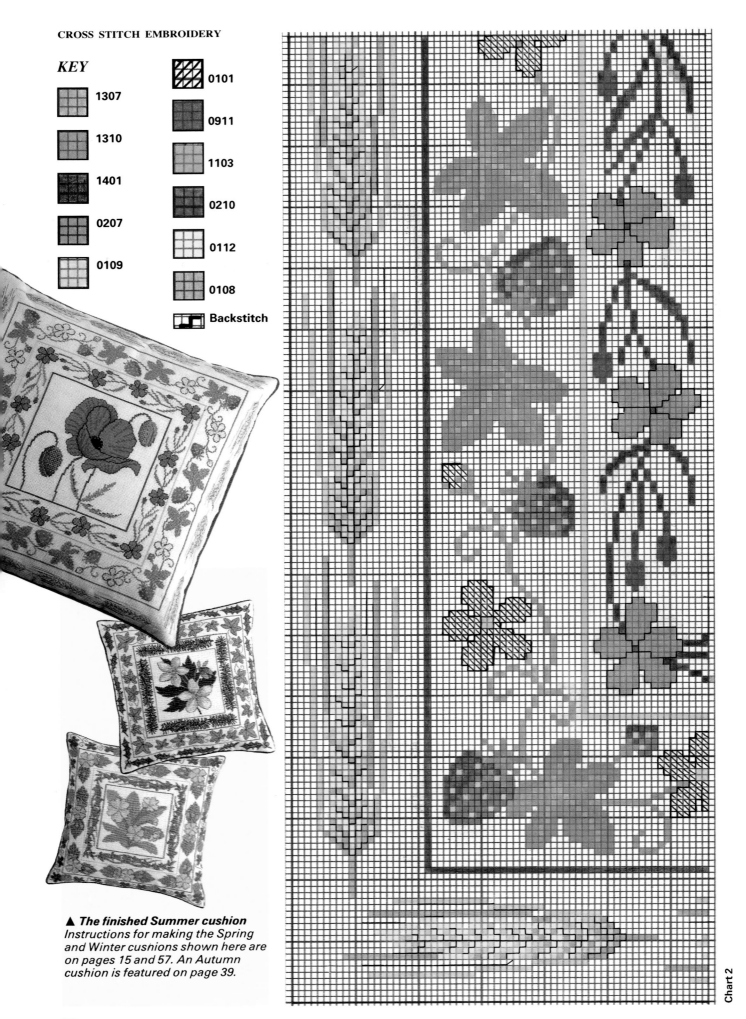

▦ 1307	▨ 0101
▦ 1310	▦ 0911
▦ 1401	▦ 1103
▦ 0207	▦ 0210
▦ 0109	▦ 0112
	▦ 0108
	▦ Backstitch

▲ The finished Summer cushion
Instructions for making the Spring and Winter cushions shown here are on pages 15 and 57. An Autumn cushion is featured on page 39.

Chart 2

Vegetable embroidery

Kitchen accessories are often overlooked as ideas for embroidery, but they offer a wealth of opportunity for unusual designs. This oven glove is embroidered with vegetable motifs – a leek, radish, mushroom and pea pod – unconventional subjects for embroidery, but just the thing for a kitchen setting.

Copy the vegetable designs from the chart on page 34, or make up your own motifs using gardening or cookery books for inspiration. Transfer the patterns to the back of the oven glove, and if you like, embroider your apron to match.

Materials
checked hardanger fabric 30 x 50cm (12 x 19 ³/₄in) with 22 threads per 2.5cm (1in). If you cannot get checked fabric, or if you want the check to match the colour of your kitchen, you can work rows of backstitch on plain fabric in the appropriate colour before you start the embroidery. If you have plain or checked cotton tea towels, buy an extra one and cut the oven glove pieces out of this. The fabric is strong enough for the oven glove, and this way you will have a co-ordinated set.

squared pattern paper each square measuring 4cm (1¹/₂in).

cotton fabric 30 x 50cm (12 x 19 ³/₄in) for the lining.

thin polyester wadding 30 x 50cm (12 x 19 ³/₄in).

cotton bias binding 2.5cm (1in) wide and 40cm (15 ³/₄in) long, to match the check on the hardanger or the colour scheme of the kitchen.

sewing thread to match the hardanger.

anchor stranded embroidery cotton one skein in each of red 19, ruby red 20, white 1, straw 891, toffee 901, lemon 292, bottle green 246, emerald 245, jade 205, lime 280, mint 214 and cinnamon 352. Use oddments of thread or your own colours if preferred.

tapestry needle no 24

▼ **Vegetable motifs**
A leek, mushroom, radish and pea pod are the inspiration for embroidery on this oven glove.

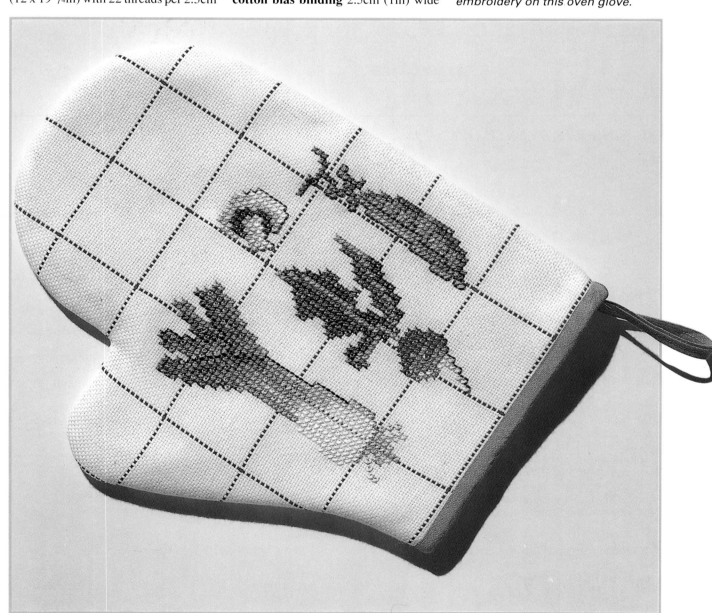

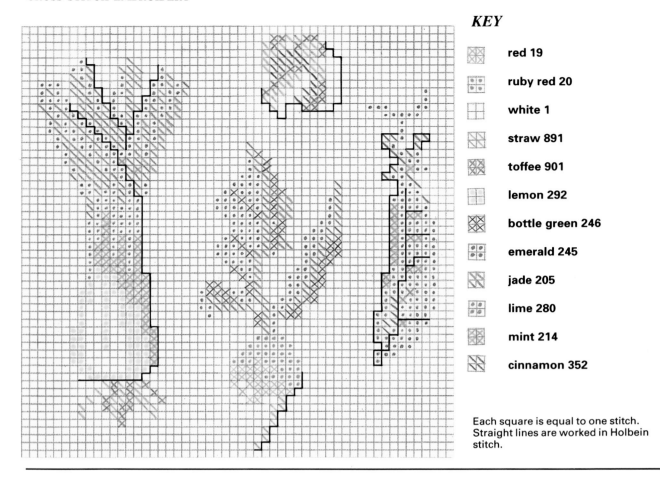

KEY

⊠	**red 19**
⊡	**ruby red 20**
⊞	**white 1**
⊠	**straw 891**
⊠	**toffee 901**
⊞	**lemon 292**
⊠	**bottle green 246**
⊡	**emerald 245**
⊠	**jade 205**
⊡	**lime 280**
⊞	**mint 214**
⊠	**cinnamon 352**

Each square is equal to one stitch. Straight lines are worked in Holbein stitch.

MAKING THE OVEN GLOVE

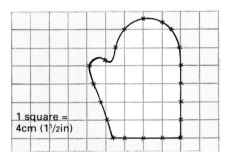

1 square = 4cm (1½in)

1 Draw up the pattern Use the diagram to draw up the pattern on squared paper. Make a cross on the pattern paper wherever the glove outline intersects with a grid line. Join up all the crosses. Place your hand over it to check for size, adjusting if necessary. Cut out the pattern.

2 Cut out the fabrics Fold the hardanger, wadding and lining fabrics in half and cut out the glove once through both layers. Leave a 1cm (³⁄₈in) seam allowance all round, except on the straight, lower edge.

3 Find centre line Only the back of the glove is embroidered so that it will not be damaged with use. Fold the back piece in half lengthwise; and run a line of tacking along the fold to mark the centre.

4 Begin the embroidery Embroider the motifs in cross stitch (see instructions on page 10) over two double squares, using three threads of stranded cotton. Position the lowest motif about 3cm (1¼in) from the lower edge.

5 Outline the motifs Using two threads of stranded cotton, work round the motifs in Holbein stitch, following the lines on the chart (see page 21). Use 901 for the mushroom, and 246 for the rest.

6 Make the glove Place front and back pieces right sides together, then place a piece of wadding either side. Stitch, taking a 1cm (³⁄₈in) seam. Snip into seam allowances for ease on curves. Turn out.

7 Loop to hang the glove Cut a length of bias binding, 12cm (4 ³⁄₄in) long. Fold in half, then edgestitch along both long edges. Fold in half to form a loop.

8 Make the lining Place the lining pieces right sides together. Sandwich the loop between the layers on the outside seam, 12mm (½in) from lower edge, raw edges matching. Pin, tack and stitch the two pieces together taking 1cm (³⁄₈in) seam.

9 Finishing off Snip into seam allowance to ease curves. Place the lining inside the glove, wrong sides together, matching seams; pin. Bind the straight raw edges with bias binding (see steps 5 and 6 on page 24).

tip

Sewing with wadding
Unless wadding is backed with another fabric, it can get caught in the feed dog on your sewing machine, making sewing both difficult and frustrating. Avoid this by backing the wadding with tissue paper, which can be ripped away after stitching.

Posy picture

This charming cross stitch picture is a lovely reminder of sunny summer days. The posy of flowers is a relatively easy project; in cross stitch outlined in Holbein stitch, it shouldn't take too much time for you to make. It is a good idea to choose a coloured frame to match one of the colours in the posy, to enhance your completed embroidery.

Materials

Cream evenweave linen 35cm (14in) square with 12 threads to 1cm (30 threads to 1in).

DMC stranded embroidery cotton 1 skein in white, delicate pink 818, rose 3326, crushed pink 335, red 326, primrose 744, sunshine 742, dandelion 741, marigold 740, sunset 946, cinnamon 301, fudge 407, fern 472, apple 471, leaf 470, forest 986, sage 3013, moss 734, yew 320, lichen 368, lilac 554, ice blue 775, forget-me-not 800, hyacinth 809, bluebell 826 and charcoal 413.

Embroidery needle size 7 and **embroidery hoop** 20cm (8in) in diameter.

Bias tape about 2m (2¼yds) to bind the embroidery hoop.

▲ Individual touch
Using simple cross stitch and outlining the work in Holbein stitch you can easily make this lovely floral posy, on a cream or white background. If you want to make the design more individual you could choose reds or pinks for your main flower colours.

35

KEY

- white
- delicate pink 818
- rose 3326
- crushed pink 335
- red 326
- primrose 744
- sunshine 742
- dandelion 741
- marigold 740
- sunset 946
- cinnamon 301
- fudge 407
- fern 472
- apple 471
- leaf 470
- forest 986
- sage 3013
- moss 734
- yew 320
- lichen 368
- lilac 554
- ice blue 775
- forget-me-not 800
- hyacinth 809
- bluebell 826
- charcoal 413

MAKING THE CROSS STITCH POSY

1 Prepare the hoop Tape the embroidery hoop and position the fabric (see page 21).

2 Marking the embroidery position Fold the fabric in half and then quarters. Press lightly and work a line of tacking stitches along the folds.

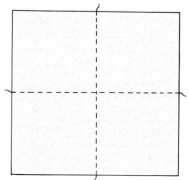

3 Working the cross stitch Match the black lines on the chart with the lines of tacking stitches to position the posy embroidery. With one square on the chart representing one stitch worked over two warp and two weft threads (see cross stitch instructions on page 10), use two strands of embroidery cotton and work in cross stitch from chart.

4 Working the Holbein stitch Using one strand of embroidery cotton, work Holbein stitch (see page 21) along the black outlines around the flowers and stems on the chart using a contrasting colour.

5 Completing the posy embroidery Remove from the frame, then press and block the embroidery before framing.

tip

A collection of posies
Using the chart as a guide for the size, you can design several other posies keeping the colour scheme similar to the original and changing the types of flowers. When completed the pictures, all framed in similar frames, will make a lovely collection.

Lavender bags

These delightful little lavender bags, decorated with a range of charming cross stitch flower motifs, are quick and easy to make. Filled with aromatic lavender, they can be tucked between freshly laundered sheets or lingerie, to infuse them with a breath of the country. Tie them with a pretty satin or velvet ribbon to bring out the vibrant colours of the embroidery.

The lavender bags make ideal gifts. You can embroider a different motif from this selection on each present, or maybe make up some of your own.

Flower motif lavender bag

Choose one of the flowers given in the charts on page 38 and a ribbon to complement the colour of the flower.

A scented collection
Once you have started making these bags you'll find it hard to stop!

MAKING THE BAGS

1 Marking the starting position Fold the fabric in half lengthways and press. Work a line of tacking stitches along the fold.

2 Embroidering the motif One square on the chart represents one stitch worked over two warp and two weft threads. Using two strands of embroidery thread, match the bold line on chart to the tacking stitches and work the first row of the chart in cross stitch, 2cm (¾in) up from the lower edge (see instructions on page 10).

3 Marking the top edge of sachet Draw a thread 5cm (2in) parallel to the top edge. Press motif.

4 Stitching the back seam With right sides together, fold the embroidery in half lengthways and stitch a 1cm (⅜in) seam along the long edges. Run your thumb nail down the seam to press open.

5 Stitching the lower seam Re-fold the fabric, so that the right sides still face, and the back seam matches the central tacking line and stitch a 1cm (⅜in) seam along the lower edge of the bag. Remove tacking stitches.

6 Stitching the sachet collar Fold the top of the sachet to wrong side along the drawn thread line and press. Using sewing thread and small running stitches, stitch the lower edge of collar in place. Turn sachet through to right side.

7 Filling the sachet Fill sachet with dried lavender to the lower edge of collar. Draw sachet together at this point and secure with a few stitches. Wind sewing thread around the neck of the sachet several times and fasten off. Trim the ends of the ribbon at angles and tie around sachet in a bow, covering the sewing thread.

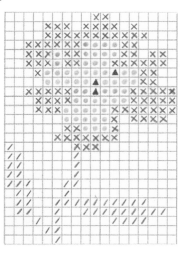

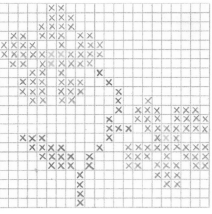

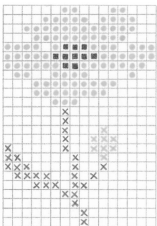

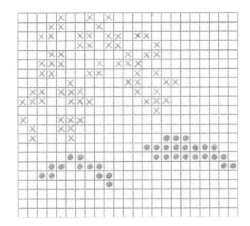

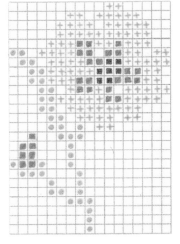

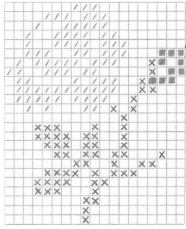

Materials
Embroidery linen 12 threads per cm (30 threads per in) off-white 16 x 19cm (6¼ x 7½in)
Anchor stranded embroidery cotton 1 skein each of colours given overleaf
Embroidery needle size 7
Sewing thread in off-white to match the colour of the linen
Velvet or **satin ribbon** 1cm (⅜in) wide and 40cm (16in) long
Dried lavender to fill bag

KEY Holbein stitch (see page 21)

Symbol	No.	Symbol	No.	Symbol	No.
✕✕	145	╱╱	210	╱╱	20
✕✕	290	✕✕	95	++	8
●●	305	■■	393	■■	5975
✕✕	817	✕✕	970	▲▲	43
●●	267	●●	969		

Autumn cushion

This cushion is the third of the seasonal designs featured in this book. Each of the four cushions spotlights the themes for that particular time of the year, and this cushion, with its frame of luscious blackberries, proclaims the start of autumn.

The fruit and fungi featured here are the ones found during the autumn months. The centre panel contains two mushrooms, and is surrounded by a rustic border of rowan leaves, then a border of ripe, juicy blackberries and finally there is an attractive outer border of acorns surrounded by oak leaves.

The embroidery is worked in quick and easy cross stitch, with finishing details in stem stitch, backstitch, straight stitch and French knots. Each of the motifs is embroidered in their true-to-life colours. All four cushions in the series are designed to be stitched on a plain, white fabric background, which helps to emphasise the wonderful colours of the embroidery.

Each of the seasonal cushions

▲ Magical warmth
Autumn is a time of rustic beauty, when the trees have rich red and yellow leaves, and brightly coloured orange and yellow berries appear. Here, our autumn cushion depicts some of these rich colours, with the bright purple blackberries and the red-tinged rowan leaves.

measures 40cm (16in) square when finished. Instructions for working the Spring, Summer and Winter cushions are on pages 15, 29 and 57.

MAKING THE CUSHION

Materials

White Aida embroidery fabric 50cm (20in) square, with 14 blocks to 2.5cm (1in)

Madeira embroidery cotton in the following colours and amounts: 2 skeins each of dark purple 0714, dark green 1602, sage green 1609 and medium green 1401, 1 skein each of dark tan 2306, dark gold 2212, tan 2011, light tan 2013, cream 2101, yellowy green 1501, pale green 1605, pink 0705, very dark green 1314 and orange 0208

Embroidery needle

Embroidery frame (optional)

Backing fabric 43cm (17in) square

Decorative cord 1.80m (2yd)

Sewing thread to match backing fabric

Cushion pad 40cm (16in) square

Scissors

Tacking thread

Note Although it's usually effortless to work Aida embroidery fabric while holding it in the hand, you will find it easier to work this design if the fabric is set into an embroidery frame. This has the advantage of leaving both hands free to work the stitches.

1 Marking the embroidery position Oversew all round the outer edges of fabric to prevent fraying. Mark the centre point along two adjacent sides of fabric. Tack straight lines from these points to form a cross that divides the fabric into quarters. The point where tacking stitches cross is the centre stitch. The embroidery can be worked in the hand or in a frame.

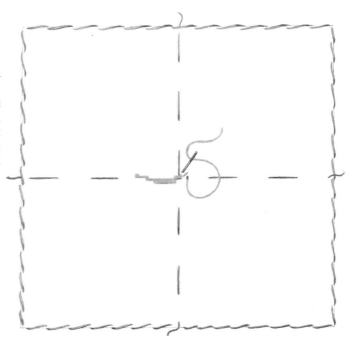

2 Beginning the embroidery Matching the centre lines on Chart 1 on page 41 with the tacked lines, begin working the embroidery on cross stitch, using two strands of embroidery cotton, with the mushroom design in the centre of the fabric. One square on Chart 1 equals one cross stitch worked over one block of fabric. Make sure that the top half of all the cross stitches face the same way. Work a border of cross stitches in dark purple 0714 all round the central motif. (For more details about cross stitch see page 10.)

3 Working the borders Once the central panel is completed you can start to work the outer borders. Following the diagram given on the left and Chart 2 on page 42 for the colours and the positioning, count the stitches and carefully embroider the outlines of the three borders with one line of cross stitch, using Madeira embroidery cotton in dark gold 2212 between the rowan and the blackberries, and then orange 0208 between the blackberries and acorns. Chart 2, on page 42, shows the borders as a strip and is turned 90° around the centre square in order to form the complete borders. This is illustrated by the broken lines in the diagram on the left. Continue to work each of the complete borders, starting from the central panel and working outwards, cross stitching first the rowan, then the blackberry and, lastly, the acorn border.

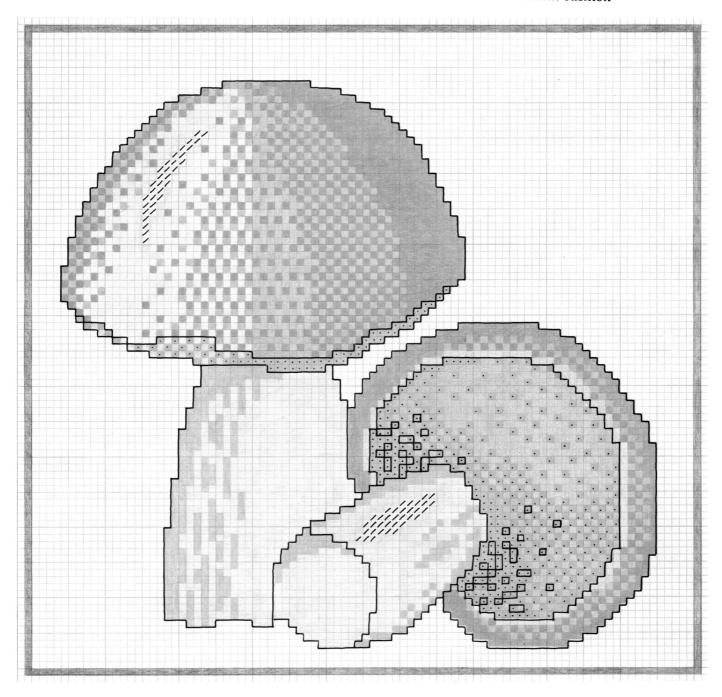

4 **Adding details** The details of the mushrooms are backstitched following the black lines on Chart 1. Use two strands of pink 0705, then backstitch round the mushroom using three strands of pink 0705.

5 **Outlining the borders** Following the black lines on Chart 2, page 42, use three strands of dark tan 2306 to stemstitch the rowan twigs, and three strands of orange 0208 to work French knots for the berries. Use three strands of cream 2101 to work cross stitches for the ground shade on the blackberries. Use three strands of dark green 1602 to work straight stitches topped with French knots for the blackberry plant stamen. Use a single strand of dark green 1314 to backstitch the acorns.

6 **Pressing the embroidery** When the embroidery is complete, remove from the embroidery frame. Steam press on the wrong side. Tack all round the outside to mark the outline.

7 **Making up** Trim down the fabric on all sides to within 2.5cm (1in) of the marked outline. Place on to the backing fabric with right sides together. Pin, tack and stitch all round, leaving an opening for the pad centrally in base edge. Trim sides and corners and then turn the cover right side out. Insert the cushion pad, turn in opening edges and pin. Hand sew cord round the cushion, along the seamline, tucking the ends of cord into the centre, then slipstitch closed.

Chart 1

KEY

▦	2306
▦	2212
▦	2011
▦	2013
▨	2101

⌐	Backstitch
⦂	French knots

KEY

■ 1314		▨ 2212	
▢ 1401		▨ 2011	
▢ 1602		▢ 2013	
▢ 1501		▨ 2101	
▢ 1609		⟋	Stem stitch
▢ 1605		✕	Cross stitch
▨ 2306		⦂	French knots
▨ 0208		⌐	Backstitch
▨ 0705		⟋	Straight stitch
▨ 0714			

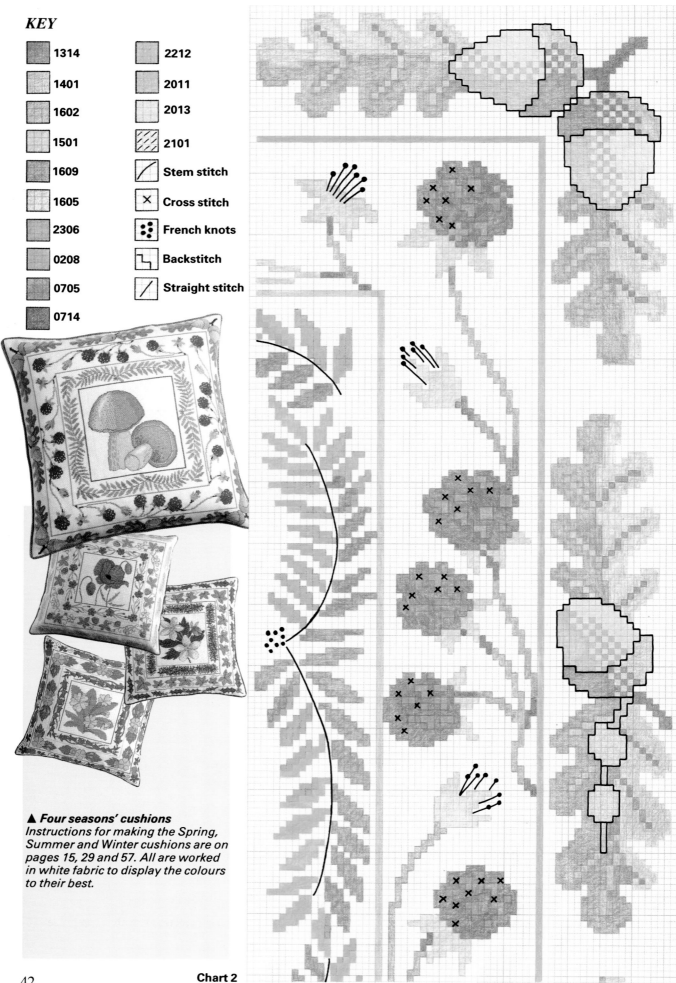

▲ Four seasons' cushions
Instructions for making the Spring, Summer and Winter cushions are on pages 15, 29 and 57. All are worked in white fabric to display the colours to their best.

Chart 2

Cat footstool

If you are a cat lover this delightful footstool is a must. Curled up after a hard night's mousing this talented tabby has, as always, found the most comfortable spot in the room – and in this case the cat looks so cosy and lifelike you may have to think twice before putting your feet up. Needlepoint is a relaxing craft to do and you will find it's a pleasure to watch the design materialise before your eyes. This tapestry is particularly simple to work using stranded wool and half cross-stitch on an open weave canvas.

▲ Paws for thought
This cat has found the ideal place to settle and will always be a comfort at your feet.

Copy our design exactly, or personalise the design by changing the colours of the background to suit your home. Fitting the tapestry on to a footstool is not difficult, but as an alternative you could back the work with toning fabric to make a cushion, or frame it into a picture.

Materials
Single interlock tapestry canvas 10 holes to 2.5cm (1in), 36cm (14in) square
Paterna tapestry wool 5 skeins daffodil 773, 4 skeins each white 260 and bluebell 342, 2 skeins each jet black 220 and camel 443, 1 skein each sand 444, stone 463, blush 875 and cream 756
Tapestry needle size 16
Readicut footstool with drop-in seat 27cm (10½in) diameter
Embroidery scissors
Iron and **ironing board**

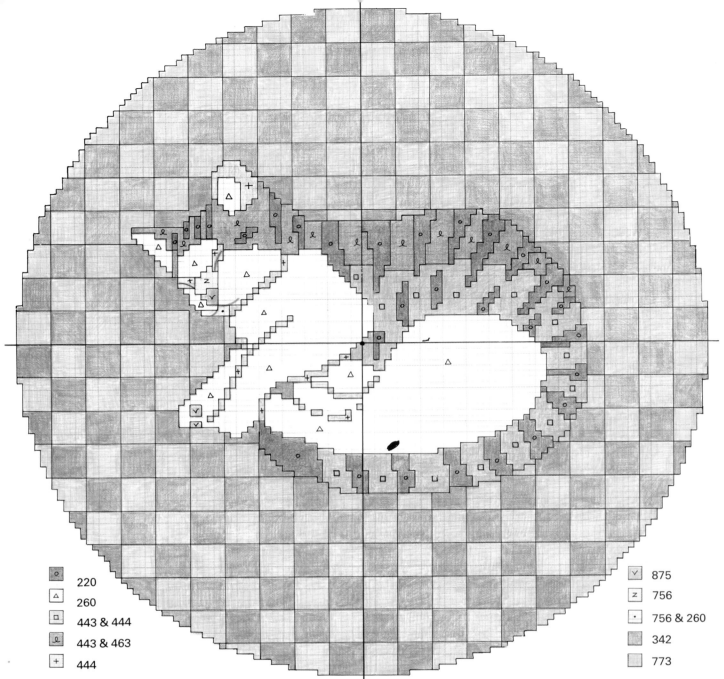

○	220
△	260
◻	443 & 444
ℓ	443 & 463
+	444

∨	875
z	756
·	756 & 260
▨	342
▢	773

MAKING THE FOOTSTOOL

1 Marking the tapestry position
Mark the centre point along two adjacent sides of the canvas. Tack straight lines from these points to form a cross and divide the canvas into quarters.

2 Stitching the cat Matching the bold lines on chart with the tacked lines, begin at the centre using 4 strands of yarn; where two colours are stated for one symbol in the key, use 2 strands of each. Work the cat in half cross-stitch following the chart. One square on the chart equals one stitch over one warp and weft thread.

3 Stitching the background Using 3 strands of tapestry yarn together, fill in the chequered background using the half cross-stitch and working in colours 773 yellow and 342 blue.

4 Adding the detail Add all the details to the tapestry using back stitch and one strand of yarn. With jet black 220 work the eyes and then highlight the cat by stitching along the edge of the face and around the front paws. Use sand 444 to complete the eyes by stitching a line above and below each eye. Embroider mouth using blush 875.

5 Block the tapestry Steam press on the wrong side of the tapestry while pulling into shape. If the canvas is still distorted, block out the work; place it face down and dampen with a spray before tacking to plywood. Allow to dry completely before removing.

6 Covering the footstool Cover the footstool with the finished tapestry using upholstery tacks or staples to hold the embroidery in place.

HALF CROSS-STITCH

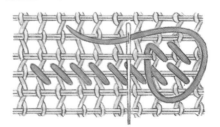

Half cross-stitch can be worked in either direction provided all diagonal stitches lie the same way. In this case the stitches go upwards from right to left. Working from right to left and keeping the needle vertical, work horizontal rows of diagonal stitches across the canvas. Following the chart, work each colour block separately making sure that you maintain an even tension to prevent the canvas showing through. Thread the yarn ends through the back of the stitches to start and finish the work.

Topiary trees

This attractive cross stitch picture depicts four stylized trees in smart decorated pots. This picture would add a rural touch hung in any room. Two distinctive tree shapes are used in the design: one with variegated leaves neatly clipped into three topiary balls; and the other a round, lollipop-shaped tree in full bloom. Each tree is divided by a neat green border dotted with tiny pink and red flowers, with a scarlet heart forming the centre.

The picture is worked over Aida fabric, which makes counting the threads for cross stitch easy. If you prefer, elements of the design can be taken from the picture and used to embellish smaller items, such as the bookmark and spectacle case featured here, or used to make smaller pictures.

The picture is approximately 32 x 18cm (12½ x 7in), the bookmark 16 x 6cm (6½ x 2½in) and spectacle case 15 x 9.5cm (6 x 3¾in).

▼ Embroidered trees
Conjure up peaceful scenes with this delightful tree embroidery. It is worked in pretty, fresh colours, and would make an attractive keepsake for family and friends.

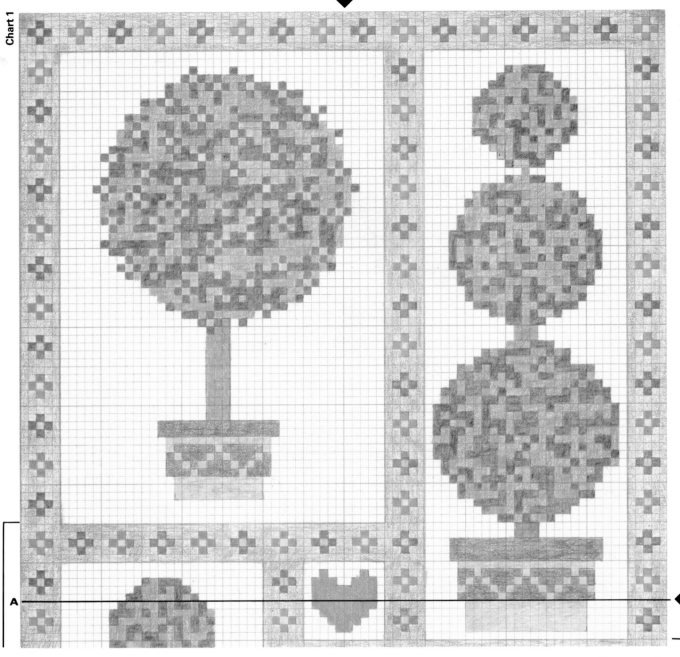

A

B

EMBROIDERED TREES

Materials
White Aida fabric 40 x 30cm (16 x 12in) with 14 blocks to 2.5cm (1in)
Anchor stranded cotton 4 skeins of laurel green 208; 2 skeins of laurel green 212; 1 skein each of scarlet 47, old rose 75, old rose 78, laurel green 206, buttercup 292, cinnamon 370, snuff brown 372 and snuff brown 374
Milward International range tapestry needle size 24
Embroidery frame (optional)
Backing board and **picture frame** to chosen size
Strong thread
Needle and **pins**

Note: Although it is usually effortless to work Aida embroidery fabric while holding it in the hand, you will find it easier to work this design if the fabric is set into an embroidery frame. Choose a rectangular frame to hold the whole design, or a round embroidery hoop which can be moved around the fabric as you work each section.

1 Preparing the fabric Oversew all round the outer edges of the fabric to prevent fraying. Measure along two adjacent sides of the fabric, and divide each measurement in half. Tack straight lines from these points to form a cross that divides the fabric into quarters. Set the fabric into an embroidery frame.

2 Matching the charts The chart for the picture has been divided into two halves. To join the charts together, match points A and B on Chart 1 above with points A and B on Chart 2 on page 47, then work the whole picture.

3 Beginning the embroidery Matching the bold black arrowheads on the charts with the tacked lines, begin working the cross stitch in the centre of the fabric, using three strands of embroidery cotton throughout. Work the picture following the chart for positioning and thread colours. Each square on the chart equals one cross stitch worked over one block. Make sure all the stitches face the same way.

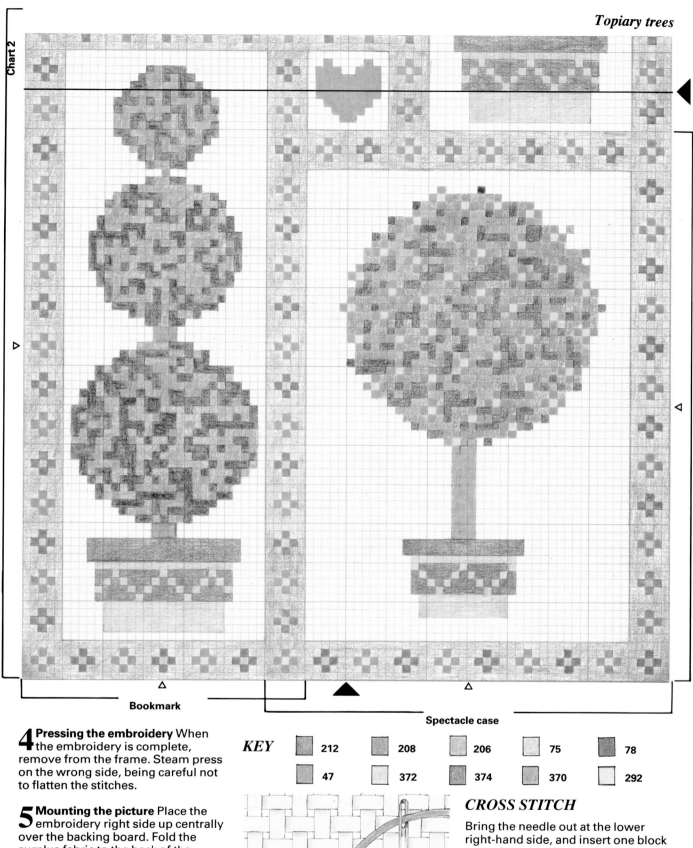

Chart 2

Bookmark

Spectacle case

4 Pressing the embroidery When the embroidery is complete, remove from the frame. Steam press on the wrong side, being careful not to flatten the stitches.

5 Mounting the picture Place the embroidery right side up centrally over the backing board. Fold the surplus fabric to the back of the board and secure at top with pins fixed into the edge of the board. Pull fabric firmly over the lower edge and pin into the board. Repeat on side edges, pulling the fabric until it lies taut on the board. Secure at the back by lacing with strong thread.

KEY

212	208	206	75	78
47	372	374	370	292

CROSS STITCH

Bring the needle out at the lower right-hand side, and insert one block up and one block to the left, forming a half cross. Continue to the end of the row, then complete the upper half as shown. Cross stitch can be worked from right to left or vice versa, but it is important that the top of all the crosses face the same way.

Bookmark and specs case

Two of the pretty tree designs in the picture have been translated into charming motifs for a smart bookmark and spectacle case.

Materials

White Aida fabric 40 x 30cm (16 x 12in) with 14 blocks to 2.5cm (1in)

Anchor stranded cotton 2 skeins of laurel green 208; 1 skein each of scarlet 47, old rose 75, old rose 78, laurel green 206, laurel green 212, buttercup 292, cinnamon 370, snuff brown 372 and snuff brown 374

Milward International range tapestry needle size 24

Backing fabric 80 x 30cm (32 x 12in)

Heavyweight fusible interfacing 40 x 30cm (16 x 12in)

BOOKMARK

1 Preparing the fabric Cut a piece of Aida fabric 25 x 15cm (10 x 6in). Oversew the outside edge to prevent fraying. Tack across centre of fabric and set into an embroidery frame.

2 Embroidering the bookmark Matching the small open arrowheads on the left-hand side of Chart 2 on page 47 with tacked lines, begin working, starting at the centre of the fabric, and using three strands of embroidery cotton. Each square on the chart equals one cross stitch worked over one block of fabric. Make sure that the top half of all the cross stitches face the same way.

3 Pressing the embroidery When the embroidery is complete, remove from the frame. Steam press on the wrong side, being careful not to flatten the stitches.

4 Making up the bookmark Cut a piece of interfacing 16 x 6cm (6½ x 2½in). Fuse centrally over wrong side of embroidery. Place the backing fabric to embroidered fabric with right sides together; stitch together following the line of the embroidery on side edges and leaving a 1.5cm (⅝in) wide border at the top and base edges. Leave an opening in one side. Trim and turn right side out. Slipstitch closed.

SPECTACLE CASE

1 Preparing the fabric Cut a piece of Aida fabric 23 x 20cm (9 x 8in). Oversew all round the outside edge to prevent fraying. Tack across the centre of the fabric in the same way as before. Set the fabric into a frame.

2 Embroidering the case Matching the small open arrowheads on the right-hand side of Chart 2 on page 47 with the tacked lines on the fabric, begin working in the centre of the fabric using three strands of embroidery cotton. One square on Chart 2 equals one cross stitch worked over one block of embroidery fabric. Embroider the spectacle case front following chart Chart 2 for position of stitches and colours. Make sure that the top half of all the cross stitches always face the same way.

3 Pressing the embroidery When all the cross stitching is complete, remove the fabric from the frame. Steam press on the wrong side, being careful not to flatten any of the cross stitches.

4 Making up the case Using the embroidered fabric as a template, cut out three pieces of backing fabric for the case back and for lining the inside. Cut a piece of heavyweight interfacing the same size as embroidered fabric and fuse to the wrong side of the fabric, matching outer edges. Place embroidery and backing fabrics with right sides together. Tack and stitch together, stitching base edges 1.5cm (⅝in) away from the embroidery, and both side edges 6mm (¼in) away from the embroidery.

5 Making up lining Place lining pieces with right sides together; stitch side and base edges leaving an opening centrally in base edges. Place lining over embroidered case with right sides together. Pin and stitch all round top edge, 1.5cm (⅝in) from embroidery. Trim and turn through opening in lining base. Turn in opening edges and slipstitch. Push lining down inside case.

Embroidered café curtain

This pretty café curtain is edged with an embroidered border inspired by a simple Shaker design, and is worked in plain stitches and traditional colours that suit the design perfectly. The border is stitched from the centre and worked outwards, enabling you to adapt the design to your curtain's width. This curtain has been designed as a straight panel to fit the window width allowing the apple tree and beehive design to be shown off to its best advantage, and not lost within any fabric folds. If your fabric is not heavy enough to hang straight,

stitching curtain weights into the hem should do the trick.

Embroidering motifs on to a plain closely woven fabric can be difficult, but here it's made easy by using purpose-made waste canvas. This is a loosely woven fabric, which can be tacked on to the right side of the curtain fabric over the motif area. Both layers of fabric are then embroidered through using the 'clearly seen' threads of the canvas as a guide to keep the stitches straight.

To complete the border Holbein stitch is then used to outline the beehives

▲ As busy as a bee
Once you have embroidered this pretty café curtain the same design could be used to decorate kitchen wall tiles and matching storage jars.

and embroider the bee's wings. Once the embroidery is finished, the waste canvas is removed to show off your beautiful embroidery with its neat stitches. Once the embroidery is completed, the curtain fabric simply needs to be hemmed and the ties stitched and attached, ready for hanging on the pole.

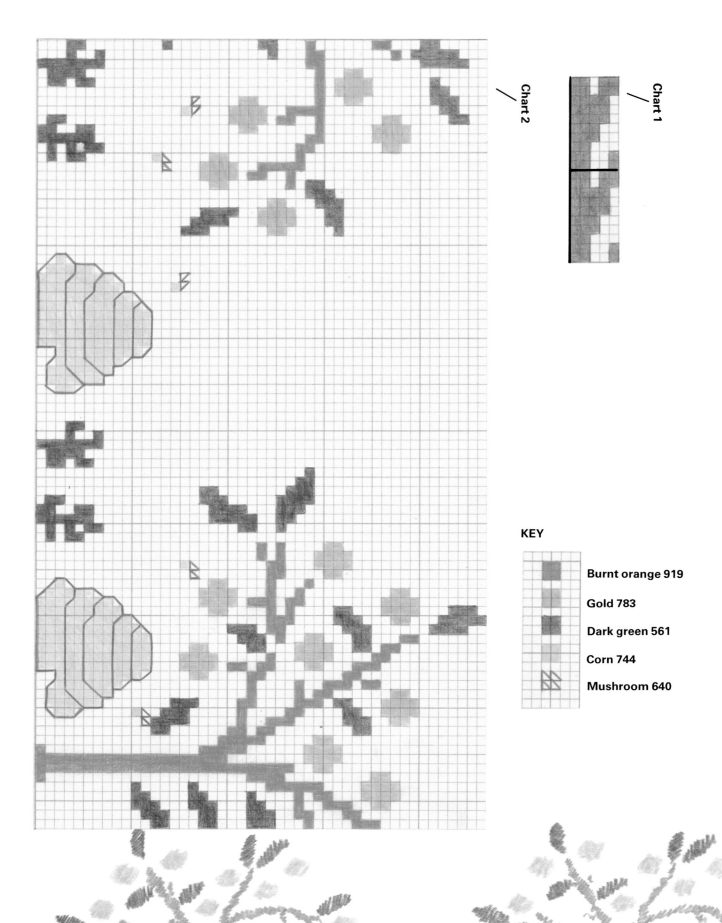

Chart 2

Chart 1

KEY

Burnt orange 919

Gold 783

Dark green 561

Corn 744

Mushroom 640

EMBROIDER THE BORDER

Materials

Cotton satin for the curtain, the width of the window plus 4cm (1½in) by the curtain depth plus 28cm (11in) for hem and seam allowance. Also strips measuring 73 x 7cm (29 x 2¾in) for each of the ties.

Zweigart waste canvas with 12 holes per 2.5cm (1in). A strip of canvas 20cm (8in) wide to fit the curtain width

DMC stranded embroidery thread 2 skeins of dark green 561 and skein each of corn 744, gold 783, burnt orange 919 and mushroom 640 for six motifs

Embroidery needle size 7

Tacking thread blue and red

Sewing thread to match fabric

Fabric scissors and **tape measure**

Plant sprayer and **tweezers** to remove waste canvas

It's best to embroider the border starting at the centre of the curtain and working outwards, accommodating the border to fit the width. Work the border strip up to the curtain edge, but each end should finish with a motif.

1 Check the curtain fabric size Using the correct fixtures, secure your curtain pole across the window in the desired position. To calculate the amount of fabric needed for the café curtain, measure the width of the curtain pole between the fixtures and add 4cm (2in) to this measurement for side hems, then measure down from the lower edge of curtain pole for the curtain length and add 28cm (11in) for both top and bottom hems. Measure your curtain fabric to check that it is the correct size for the window.

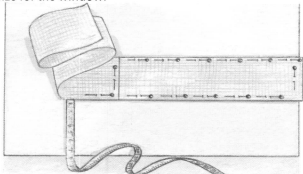

2 Attach the waste fabric Pin the strip of waste canvas across the right side of the curtain fabric placing it 18cm (7in) up from the lower edge, overlap the ends at joins as necessary. Using small stitches and the blue thread, tack the canvas in place around the edges.

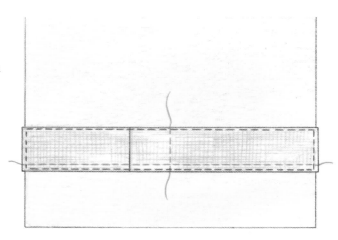

3 Mark the embroidery position Fold the curtain fabric in half lengthways and tack a line of red stitches across the canvas along the fold. Tack another line of red stitches along the waste canvas, 23cm (9in) up from the lower edge of the curtain fabric.

4 Cross stitch the border edging Match the red tacking stitches on the curtain with the bold lines given on chart 1 on page 50. Then using the threads of the waste canvas as a guide for the stitch size, work the design in cross stitch through both layers of fabric using 2 strands of embroidery thread in the appropriate colour. Continue to embroider the green border edging by repeating the complete chart, working out towards the side edges and finishing at least 3cm (1in) from the edges (for cross stitch detail see page 10).

5 Embroider the border Match the bold lines given on chart 2 on page 50 with the tacking stitches as before and use 2 strands of embroidery thread and cross stitch to embroider the chart directly above the green edging. Repeat the design across the fabric, finishing with a complete motif, either a beehive or a tree, before the end of the border edging.

6 Complete the embroidery Using 1 strand of embroidery thread, mushroom 640, and Holbein stitch, outline the beehives and work the bee's wings as shown on the chart (for details of how to work Holbein stitch see page 21).

7 Remove the waste fabric Dampen the right side of the waste fabric with a fine spray of water from the plant sprayer. Leave for a couple of minutes until the canvas has softened, then use the tweezers to carefully remove the canvas threads, one at a time; spray the fabric with more moisture if necessary.

MAKING THE CAFE CURTAIN

1 **Hem the side edges** Press the fabric to remove any creases. Fold a double hem measuring 1cm (½in) wide to wrong side along one side edge. Pin, then slipstitch hem in place and press. Repeat for other side.

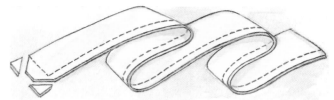

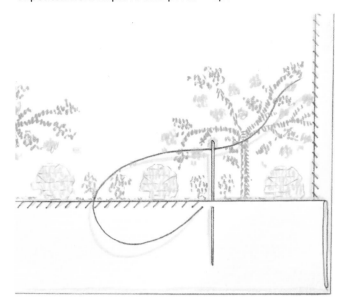

2 **Hem the lower edge** Fold a double hem measuring a finished depth of 7.5cm (3in) to the wrong side along the lower edge, matching the hem fold to the straight edge of the green strip within the border pattern. Pin, then slipstitch the hem in place. Neatly slipstitch each end of hem closed.

3 **Calculate the amount of ties required** Measure the width of the curtain and work out how many ties will be needed if they are spaced about 12cm (5in) apart and there is one at each end. Cut the required number of ties, each measuring 73 x 7cm (29 x 2¾in).

4 **Make the ties** With right sides together, fold each tie in half lengthways. Using straight stitch, sew a 1cm (⅜in) seam along one short end and the long edge. Trim the seams and snip the seam allowance at the corners. Turn tie to right side and press. Turn the raw edges at end to inside of tie and neatly slipstitch the open end of the tie closed.

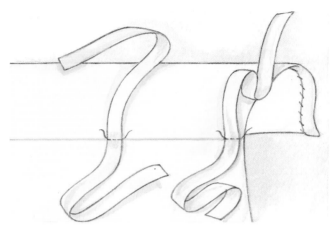

5 **Attach the ties to the curtain** Hold the curtain up against the window to check the length, then fold over the top edge and press. Fold the ties in half widthways and press. Matching the folds on the ties to the fold along the top edge of the curtain, place one tie at each end with the edge of the tie to the edge of the curtain, then position the others evenly spaced between. You may need to make it slightly less, or more, than 12cm (5in). Pin, tack then machine stitch the ties in place stitching along the fold.

6 **Finish off** Fold the pressed top hem to the wrong side and turn under the raw edges to make a double hem then slipstitch in place. Slipstitch the hem ends closed. Press curtain, then tie on to pole.

◄ *Honey-pots*
This lovely café curtain is sewn in traditional colours, which are ideal for a Shaker style kitchen. The motif is so stylish, it could also be embroidered on more than one fabric around the room. Using white fabric with coloured embroidery threads is not a problem they are both machine washable.

Embroidered bedlinen

T otally enchanting, this duvet cover and pillowcase are strewn with tiny embroidered flowers which decorate this clever combination of pink gingham and crisp white cotton.

The embroidery fabric is marked into large squares by withdrawing fabric threads and weaving lengths of pearl pink embroidery cotton through the material to take its place. Delightful flower motifs are then worked in simple cross stitch in the centre of each large square. A selection of seven flower

motifs are charted on page 56 so you can either use the same one in each square or embroider a variety of designs over the cover. The pillowcase is decorated in the same way.

Easy to sew, yet very practical, flap fastenings hold the pillow and duvet in their covers and pretty pink ribbons can also be added to hold the opening closed. This duvet cover measures 140 x 200cm (55 x 80in), suitable for a single size duvet. The pillowcase measures 75 x 58cm (30 x 23in).

▲ Covered in flowers
Crisp white cotton fabric embroidered with a pretty pink check and delicate flowers make an attractive cover for this bed. The parallel pink lines are formed by withdrawing fabric threads and weaving in pearl cotton.

Here we have used pink gingham fabric for a contrasting backing, but if you want to change the colour scheme to match your bedroom use different coloured gingham and embroidery threads to match.

MAKING THE COVER

Materials

White evenweave fabric 2.5m (2¾yd) of 140cm (55in) wide with 25 threads to 2.5cm (1in)

Pink and white gingham fabric 2m (2¼yd) of 140cm (55in) wide

DMC stranded embroidery cotton one skein in each of the colours indicated in the key on page 56.

DMC pearl cotton No 5 in light pink and **tapestry needle**

Ribbon or **decorative braid** 1.40m (1⅝yd) of 1.5cm (⅝in) wide

Sewing thread and **needle**

1 Planning the background The grid background is formed by withdrawing threads vertically and horizontally from the embroidery fabric to form large squares. First withdraw the threads down the length of the fabric. Start by measuring 10cm (4in) from one selvedge edge and mark; this will be the first withdrawn thread.

Following chart A, continue to measure across the fabric, first 24cm (9½in) then 9cm (3½in). This will form large panels, divided by narrow parallel strips. Carefully mark off the threads as you measure them, either with a soft pencil or a tacking thread.

2 Withdrawing the threads Using a blunt tapestry needle lift the first marked thread away from the fabric. Gently pull the thread out of the fabric. Repeat with each marked thread. This will leave empty channels in the fabric.

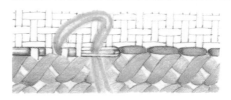

7 Adding a back stitch outline Once the motif is complete, use two strands of embroidery cotton to back-stitch round the flower following the dark lines on the diagram on page 56. Pick the darkest embroidery cotton used in the flower motif for the backstitching. Repeat, to embroider a motif centrally in each square.

8 Making up the duvet Turn under a double 1cm (⅜in) hem along base edge of embroidered fabric; pin and stitch hem. Stitch a hem in the same way along base edge of gingham fabric. Place gingham fabric to embroidered fabric with right sides facing and raw edges together. To form the holding flap, turn the excess embroidered fabric over hem edge of gingham fabric; pin and stitch sides and across top edge, taking 1.5cm (⅝in) seam allowance. Trim and neaten all raw edges. Turn duvet cover right side out, tucking holding flap inside.

THE PILLOWCASE

Materials

White evenweave fabric 96.5 x 63.5cm (38 x 25in) with 25 threads to 2.5cm (1in)

Pink and white gingham 81 x 63.5cm (32 x 25in)

DMC Embroider cotton

DMC pearl cotton No 5 in light pink and **tapestry needle**

Sewing thread and **needle**

1 Embroidering the fabric Measure and mark the threads to be withdrawn, following chart B. Withdraw the threads and weave with pink embroidery cotton as for duvet cover. Embroider a different motif in each square.

◀ *Choosing the fabric*
This pretty duvet set was embroidered over an unusual fabric, woven with alternate squares to create a chequered effect. We have chosen to use an evenweave fabric as it is readily available and easy to embroider.

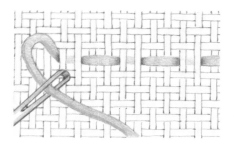

3 **Weaving the check** Thread the tapestry needle with a length of pink cotton slightly longer than the fabric, then working under and over alternate pairs of fabric threads, weave the pink pearl cotton thread along each channel in the fabric.

4 **Completing the background** When all the vertical lines are complete, mark and withdraw the horizontal lines across the fabric, to create the square grid effect. Follow chart A to position each set of lines. Finish by weaving the pearl cotton thread along each channel, as before, neatly crossing over the vertical lines where they intersect.

5 **Marking motif positions** Measure and mark the centre of each large square with a line of tacking stitches. These will match the black lines on the motif diagrams (see page 56).

6 **Embroidering the motifs** Each motif is worked in cross stitch using three strands of embroidery cotton worked over two threads of fabric. Pick one of the motifs from the diagram and using tacking stitches as a guide, embroider centrally in first square.

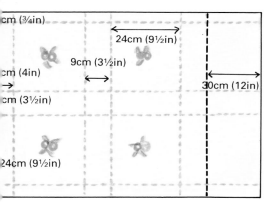

9 **Adding the ties** Cut ribbon into eight equal lengths. Mark the positions for ties equally spaced along the edge. Sew pairs of ribbon to either side. Turn under one end of each ribbon and handsew just inside opening. Cut ribbon ends diagonally.

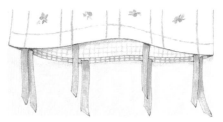

▲ *Chart B: Pillowcase*
▶ *Chart A: Duvet cover*

2 **Making up pillowcase** Pin and stitch a double 1cm (⅜in) wide hem along one long edge of checked gingham fabric. Repeat to stitch a double hem on flap end of embroidered fabric. Place checked fabric to embroidered fabric with right sides together, raw edges matching. Fold the excess embroidered fabric over gingham side of pillowcase. Pin and stitch sides and end, taking 1.5cm (⅝in) seam allowance. Neaten raw edges. Turn pillowcase right side out, tucking the flap inside.

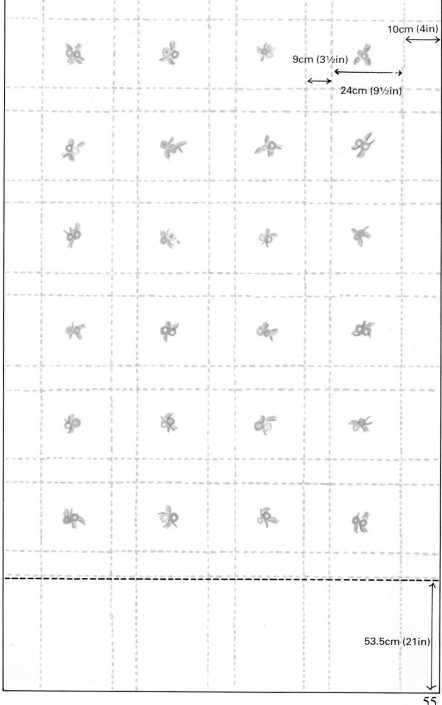

FLOWER MOTIF CHART

Each square equals one cross stitch over two threads of fabric.

KEY

		321			351			353			601			603			605
		606			608			701			704			900			

56

Winter cushion

This cushion is the fourth in a series of seasonal designs for cushions that illustrate the gardens and hedgerows of a particular time of the year.

The centre panel of this winter design features a creamy-white Christmas rose and is surrounded with borders of dark green yew, a row of swirling variegated ivy and finally an outer border of holly . As for the other three cushions in this series the embroidery is worked mainly in cross stitch, with the details in French knots and backstitch. Each motif is embroidered in its true-to-life colours and all four cushions in the series have a plain white fabric background. The finished cushion measures 40cm (16in) square.

▼ Seasonal choice
Here, the delightful floral embroidery has been made into a cushion, but it would look equally good framed up as a picture. As part of the background can be left unstitched the design will grow quickly and easily, creating a pretty keepsake of the flowers and foliage found in abundance during the winter.

EMBROIDERING THE CUSHION

Materials

Aida embroidery fabric 50cm (20in) square with 14 blocks to 2.5cm (1in)

Madeira embroidery cotton in the following colours and amounts: 5 skeins medium green 1404, 2 skeins each of dark green 1705, bright green 1307, green 1305, lime 1410, 1 skein each of very dark green 1505, pale green 1409, deep purple 0810, pale purple 0809, yellow 0109, orange 0207, red 0212 and cream 0101

Embroidery needle size 24

Embroidery frame (optional)

Backing fabric 43cm (17in) square

Decorative cord 1.80m (2yd) to match backing fabric or in one of the main colours in the embroidery

Sewing thread to match backing fabric

Cushion pad 40 cm (16in) square

Note: Although it's usually effortless to work Aida embroidery fabric holding it in the hand, you will find it easier to work this design if the fabric is set into an embroidery frame. This has the advantage of leaving both hands free to work the stitches.

1 Marking the embroidery position Oversew all round the outer edges of the fabric to prevent fraying. Mark the centre point along two adjacent sides of the fabric. Tack straight lines from these points to form a cross that divides the fabric into quarters. The point where the tacking stitches cross is the centre stitch. The embroidery can be worked in the hand or set into an embroidery frame (see *Note* above).

2 Beginning the embroidery Matching the bold black lines on chart 1 on page 59 with the tacked lines, begin working the cross stitch embroidery in the centre of the fabric using two strands of emroidery cotton. One square on chart 1 equals one cross stitch over one block of fabric. Work the centre panel first following chart 1 for the position of the stitches and thread colours. Make sure the top half of all the cross stitches face the same way. Work a border in orange 0207 all round the central motif. (For cross stitch see page 10).

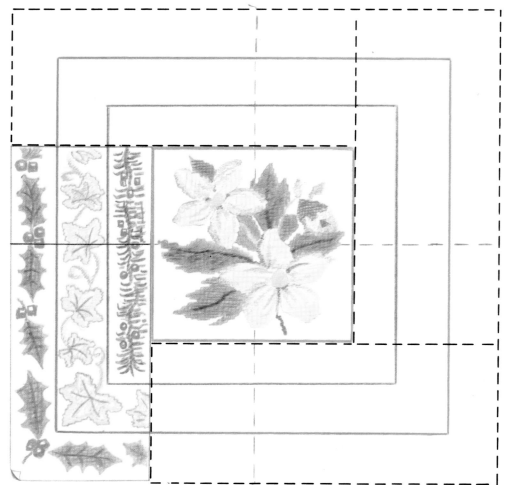

3 Working the borders Following the diagram left and chart 2 on page 60 count the stitches and embroider the outlines of the three borders with one line of cross stitch, using Deep Purple 0810 between the yew and ivy leaves and Red 0212 between ivy leaves and holly. Chart 2, on page 60, is turned 90° around the centre square to form the complete borders, as shown by the broken lines in the diagram. Work the complete borders outwards from the central panel, following chart 2 for the colour and placement of the stitches for yew, ivy and holly leaves. One square on chart 2 equals one cross stitch worked over one block of fabric. Work the complete yew border first, then the ivy border and finally the border of holly leaves and berries all round the outer edge. Again, check that the top half of all the cross stitches are worked so that they are all facing in the same direction.

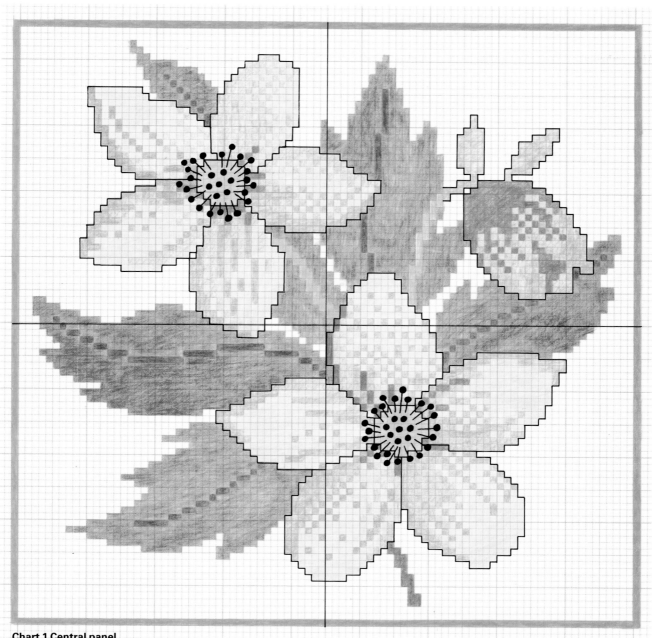

Chart 1 Central panel

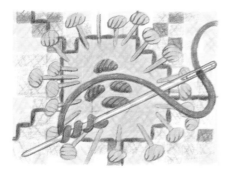

4 **Adding details to the roses** Work outline and details following the black lines on chart 1. Use a single strand of 1505 to backstitch round petals. Work French knots on the outer edge for stamen heads using three strands of 0109 and 1810 for central French knots. Use two strands of 0109 for straight stitched stamens. (For French knots see page 13).

5 **Outlining the borders** Following the black lines on chart 2, on page 60, use two strands of bright green 1305 to backstitch round the yew branches, two strands of medium green 1404 to backstitch the outlines and veins on the ivy leaves and two strands of very dark green 1505 to backstitch round the holly berries on the outer border.

KEY

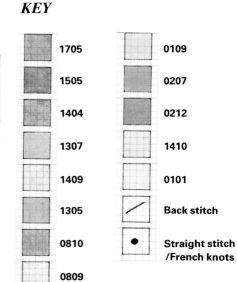

▨	1705	▨	0109
▨	1505	▨	0207
▨	1404	▨	0212
▨	1307	▨	1410
▨	1409	▨	0101
▨	1305	/	Back stitch
▨	0810	•	Straight stitch /French knots
▨	0809		

59

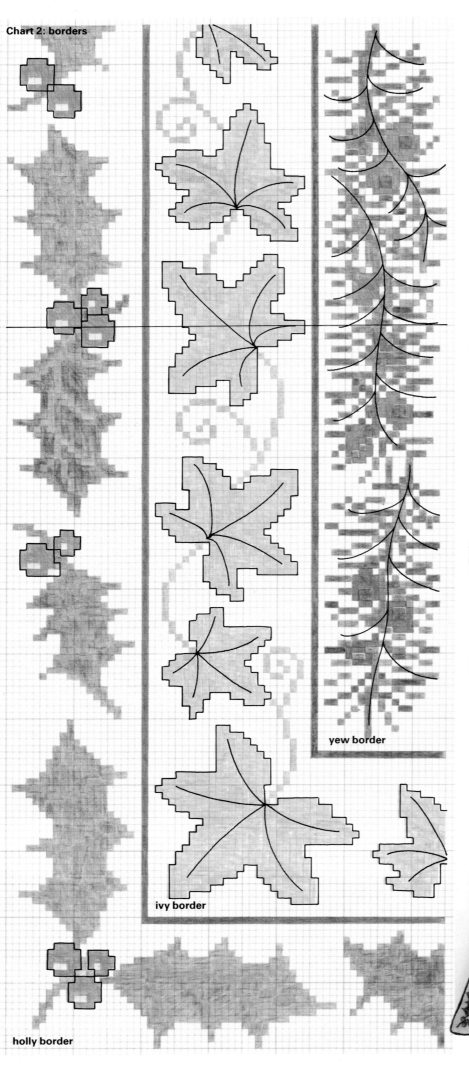

Chart 2: borders

yew border

ivy border

holly border

6 **Pressing the embroidery** When the embroidery is complete, remove from the frame. Steam press on the wrong side, being careful not to flatten the stitches. Tack all round the outside to mark the outline.

7 **Making up the cushion** Trim down the fabric on all sides to within 2.5cm (1in) of the marked outline. Place to the backing fabric with right sides together. Pin, tack and stitch all round the cushion cover, leaving an opening centrally in base edge, for turning and filling. Trim sides and corners and turn cover right side out. Insert cushion pad. Turn in opening edges and pin and tack together.

8 **Adding the cord** Handsew cord all round the seamline of the cushion. Tuck the raw ends of the cord into the centre of the tacked opening.

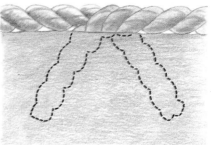

9 **Finishing off** Slipstitch opening edges together to close, catching in cord. Catch the cord invisibly together at the opening.

◀ *Chart 2*
This chart shows a section of the borders. Each square on the chart equals one cross stitch.